Becoming a U.S. Citizen through Derivative Citizenship

A Step-by-Step Guide to Understanding Your Path to U.S. Citizenship by Derivation

Attorney Brian D. Lerner

LAW OFFICES OF
BRIAN D. LERNER
A PROFESSIONAL CORPORATION

ATTORNEY DRAFTED IMMIGRATION PETITIONS

By

Brian D. Lerner
Attorney at Law

Disclaimer and Terms of Use:

ISBN: 978-1-958990-64-3

TABLE OF CONTENTS

INTRODUCTION

There are a multitude of different immigration petitions and applications. They are complex and full of requirements. Obviously it would be best to hire an immigration attorney to best prepare the petitions and applications. However, this can certainly cost thousands of dollars.

The next best option is to get a sample of the petition written by an experienced immigration attorney. The samples cost a fraction of what would be charged by an immigration attorney. However, while the reader has to alter, amend and change the parts of the sample petition to reflect their actual situation, it is a fantastic roadmap for them to use. If the reader has purchased the entire petition or application, they will have real live samples of cover letters, forms, declarations, affidavits and the necessary exhibits to use. The samples come from real cases and the names of those clients have been redacted to protect the privacy of that person or corporation.

These are petitions and applications that have been drafted by an experienced immigration attorney with over 25 years of experience. Get the benefits of that experience without the costs.

The Law Offices of Brian D. Lerner, APC. The law practice consists of Immigration and Nationality Law and everything involved with and regarding immigration which includes citizenship, investment visas, family and employment visas, removal and deportation hearings, appeals, waivers, adjustment, consulate processing and all types of immigration and citizenship matters. Thousands of families have been reunited and/or permitted to stay in the U.S. and/or return to the U.S. because of the successful work of Immigration Attorney Brian D. Lerner.

This law office handles all types of immigration cases including family based and employment based. Immigration issues range from immigration court proceedings to trying to fix what paralegals may have done that was neither correct nor proper. Foreign nationals must have experienced lawyers admitted to practice law.

The Law Offices of Brian D. Lerner, APC, handles cases arising from business visas, work permits, Green Cards, non-immigrant visas, deportation, citizenship, appeals and all areas of immigration. The Law Offices of Brian D. Lerner, APC does EB-5 Investor Visas, H-1B Specialty Occupation, L-1 Intracompany Transferee, E-2 Treaty Investor, E-1 Treaty Trader, O-1 Extraordinary Ability among others. Regarding immigrant visas for the Green Card, the firm does PERM and advanced degree PERM, Family Petitions, and Extraordinary Alien Petitions. In addition to affirmative petitions, the Law Firm represents people in people in deportation and removal hearings, including political asylum, withholding of removal, and convention against torture cases.

Brian D. Lerner has been certified as an expert in Immigration & Nationality Law by the California State Bar, Board of Legal Specialization since 2000 and has been re-certified three times. He now passes on his decades of experience by allowing the Reader, Law Schools, Professors and other Immigration Attorneys to purchase sample petitions on every facet of Immigration Law.

About Derivative Citizenship Application

Derivative citizenship is citizenship given to children through the naturalization of parents or, sometimes, foreign-born children adopted by United States citizen parents, if certain conditions are met.

September 11, 2013

USCIS
Attn: Form N-600
1820 E. Skyharbor Circle S. Suite 100
Phoenix. AZ. 85034

Re: ███████████████████████

   Application for Certificate of Citizenship

Dear Officer:

The above-referenced applicant hereby submits the following documents in support of his application Derivative Citizenship. Also enclosed are the money orders for the $600 application fee.

FORMS	DESCRIPTIONS
Form G-28	Notice of Entry of Appearance as Attorney or Representative;
Form G-1145	e-Notification of Application
Form N-600	Application for Certificate of Citizenship

TABLE OF EXIBITS

EXIBITS:	DESCRIPTIONS
"1"	Applicant's Birth Certificate with English Translation;
"2"	Applicant's Identification Card ;
"3"	Father's Certificate of Naturalization;
"4"	Father's Declaration;
"5"	Proof of Support provided by Father to Applicant as Evidence Of Paternity;
"6"	Photos Showing Relationship of Applicant and his Father;
"7"	Mother's Death Certificate with English Translation;
"8"	Copy of High School Diploma;
"9"	Copy of Authorization to Act as a Solo Parent;
"10"	Copy of High School Student registration.

I.
INTRODUCTION

Applicant, through counsel, submits the following brief in support of his application for a Derivative Citizenship. Applicant qualifies for United States citizenship through his father ██████████████████ pursuant to section 320(a) of the Immigration and Nationality Act as amended by Title I, section 101(a) of the Child Citizenship Act of 2000.

II.
FACTS

Applicant was born out-of-wedlock to █████████████████████████ on May 23, 1983. His father was petition by his Grandfather and was awarded of Certificate of Naturalization on April 30, 1983; it was a month before the applicant was born. See Applicant's Birth Certificate and Father's Certificate of Naturalization, See **EXHIBIT 1 and 3**

III.
REQUIREMENTS FOR AUTOMATIC ACQUISITION OF CITIZENSHIP

Since the Child Citizenship Act of 2000 took effect, it no longer requires the applicant to prove the divorce of his parents if he is in custody of one parent. **See EXHIBIT 10**. Under 8 CFR 320.2 a person automatically becomes a US citizen when:

> *"320.2(a) General. To be eligible for citizenship under section 320*
> *of the Act, a person must establish that the following conditions*
> *have been met after February 26, 2001:*
> *320.2(a)(1) The child has at least one United States citizen parent*
> *(by birth or naturalization);*
> *320.2(a)(2) The child is under 18 years of age; and*
> *320.2(a)(3) The child is residing in the United States in the legal*
> *and physical custody of the United States citizen parent, pursuant*
> *to a lawful admission for permanent residence."*

A. FATHER'S APPLICANT IS A NATURALIZED UNITED STATES CITIZENS

Under the Child Citizenship Act of 2000 it requires the child to have at least one parent that is a United States citizen parent, the citizenship can either be by birth or naturalization. In this case the father's applicant is a naturalized citizen. And given that, the applicant satisfies the first requirement thru his father. Since applicant's father became a naturalized citizen on April 30, 1983. See **EXHIBIT 3.**

B. APPLICANT WAS UNDER 18 YEARS OLD WHEN THE FIRST AND THIRD REQUIREMENT WAS MET

The law requires that the child must be under 18 years old for applicant to automatically acquire citizenship. In this case the applicant was not yet born when his father became a naturalized United States citizen. See **EXHIBIT 1 and 3.**

C. APPLICANT IS IN THE LEGAL AND PHYSICAL CUSTODY OF HIS PARENT

The law requires that the child be in the legal and physical custody of the United States citizen parent as a lawful permanent resident. In the present case, applicant who was 14 years old when he entered the United States with his father who was a naturalized citizen and as lawful permanent resident. See **EXHIBIT 10**. The definition of legal custody is found in under 8 CFR 320.1:

> "*Legal custody refers to the responsibility for and authority over a child.*
>
> *(1) For the purpose of the CCA, the Service will presume that a U.S. citizen parent has legal custody of a child, and will recognize that U.S. citizen parent as having lawful authority over the child, absent evidence to the contrary, in the case of:*
>
> *(i) A biological child who currently resides with both natural parents (who are married to each other, living in marital union, and not separated),*
>
> *(ii) A biological child who currently resides with a surviving natural parent (if the other parent is deceased), or*
>
> *(iii) In the case of a biological child born out of wedlock who has been legitimated and currently resides with the natural* **parent.**"

Applicant falls under item *ii*, since his parent was never married and he stay with father who was a naturalized U.S. citizen. Section 101(b)(1)(C) of the Immigration and Nationality Act states:

> "*a child legitimated under the law of the child's residence or domicile, or under the law of the father's residence or domicile, whether in or outside the United States, if such legitimation takes place before the child reaches the age of eighteen years and the child is in the legal custody of the legitimating parent or parents at the time of such legitimation;*"

V.
CONCLUSION

Base on the foregoing, the applicant meets all the conditions under section 320(a) of the Immigration and Nationality Act. Applicant respectfully request for his application for a United States passport be approved.

Please contact our office at (562) 495-0554, if you have any questions or require additional information.

Sincerely,

Brian D. Lerner
Attorney at Law

FORM G-28:
Notice of Appearance as Attorney or Accredited Representative

Notice of Entry of Appearance
as Attorney or Accredited Representative
Department of Homeland Security

DHS
Form G-28
OMB No. 1615-0105
Expires 02/29/2016

Part 1. Information About Attorney or Accredited Representative

Name and Address of Attorney or Accredited Representative

1.a. Family Name *(Last Name)*

1.b. Given Name *(First Name)*

1.c. Middle Name

2. Name of Law Firm or Recognized Organization

3. Name of Law Student or Law Graduate

4. State Bar Number

5.a. Street Number

5.b. Street Name

5.c. Apt. ☐ Ste. ☐ Flr. ☐

5.d. City or Town

5.e. State ▼ **5.f.** Zip Code

5.g. Postal Code

5.h. Province

5.i. Country

6. Daytime Phone Number ( ) -

7. E-Mail Address of Attorney or Accredited Representative

Part 2. Eligibility Information For Attorney or Accredited Representative

(Check applicable items(s) below)

1. ☐ I am an attorney eligible to practice law in, and a member in good standing of, the bar of the highest court(s) of the following State(s), possession(s), territory(ies), commonwealth(s), or the District of Columbia.

1.a.

1.b. I *(choose one)* ☐ *am not* ☐ *am*
subject to any order of any court or administrative agency disbarring, suspending, enjoining, restraining, or otherwise restricting me in the practice of law. (If you are subject to any order(s), explain fully in the space below.)

1.b.1.

2. ☐ I am an accredited representative of the following qualified nonprofit religious, charitable, social service, or similar organization established in the United States, so recognized by the Department of Justice, Board of Immigration Appeals pursuant to 8 CFR 292.2. Provide the name of the organization and the expiration date of accreditation.

2.a. Name of Recognized Organization

2.b. Date Accreditation expires *(mm/dd/yyyy)* ▶

3. ☐ I am associated with

3.a.

the attorney or accredited representative of record who previously filed Form G-28 in this case, and my appearance as an attorney or accredited representative is at his or her request. If you check this item, also complete **number 1 (1.a. - 1.b.1.) or number 2 (2.a. - 2.b.) in Part 2** *(whichever is appropriate)*.

4. ☐ I am a law student or law graduate working under the direct supervision of the attorney or accredited representative of record on this form in accordance with the requirements in 8 CFR 292.1(a)(2)(iv).

Part 3. Notice of Appearance as Attorney or Accredited Representative

This appearance relates to immigration matters before (select one):

1. ☐ USCIS - List the form number(s)

1.a. [   ]

2. ☐ ICE - List the specific matter in which appearance is entered

2.a. [   ]

3. ☐ CBP - List the specific matter in which appearance is entered

3.a. [   ]

I hereby enter my appearance as attorney or accredited representative at the request of:

4. **Select only one:** ☐ Applicant   ☐ Petitioner
   ☐ Respondent (ICE, CBP)

Name of Applicant, Petitioner, or Respondent

5.a. Family Name
     (Last Name) [   ]

5.b. Given Name
     (First Name) [   ]

5.c. Middle Name [   ]

5.d. Name of Company or Organization, if applicable
     [   ]

NOTE: Provide the mailing address of Petitioner, Applicant, or Respondent and not the address of the attorney or accredited representative, **except when a safe mailing address is permitted** on an application or petition filed with Form G-28.

6.a. Street Number
     and Name [   ]

6.b. Apt. ☐   Ste. ☐   Flr. ☐ [   ]

6.c. City or Town [   ]

6.d. State [▾]   6.e. Zip Code [   ]

7. Provide A-Number and/or Receipt Number

[   ]

Pursuant to the Privacy Act of 1974 and DHS policy, I hereby consent to the disclosure to the named Attorney or Accredited Representative of any record pertaining to me that appears in any system of records of USCIS, ICE, or CBP.

8.a. Signature of Applicant, Petitioner, or Respondent

[   ]

8.b. Date   *(mm/dd/yyyy)* ▶ [   ]

Part 4. Signature of Attorney or Accredited Representative

I have read and understand the regulations and conditions contained in 8 CFR 103.2 and 292 governing appearances and representation before the Department of Homeland Security. I declare under penalty of perjury under the laws of the United States that the information I have provided on this form is true and correct.

1. Signature of Attorney or Accredited Representative

[   ]

2. Signature of Law Student or Law Graduate

[   ]

3. Date   *(mm/dd/yyyy)* ▶ [   ]

Part 5. Additional Information

1.
[   ]
[   ]
[   ]
[   ]
[   ]
[   ]
[   ]
[   ]
[   ]
[   ]
[   ]
[   ]

FORM G-1145:

E-Notification of Application

e-Notification of Application/Petition Acceptance

Department of Homeland Security

U.S. Citizenship and Immigration Services

USCIS

Form G-1145

What Is the Purpose of This Form?

Use this form to request an electronic notification (e-Notification) when U.S. Citizenship and Immigration Services accepts your immigration application. This service is available for applications filed at a USCIS Lockbox facility.

General Information

Complete the information below and clip this form to the first page of your application package. You will receive one e-mail and/or text message for each form you are filing.

We will send the e-Notification within 24 hours after we accept your application. Domestic customers will receive an e-mail and/or text message; overseas customers will only receive an e-mail. Undeliverable e-Notifications cannot be resent.

The e-mail or text message will display your receipt number and tell you how to get updated case status information. It will not include any personal information. The e-Notification does not grant any type of status or benefit; rather it is provided as a convenience to customers.

USCIS will also mail you a receipt notice (I-797C), which you will receive within 10 days after your application has been accepted; use this notice as proof of your pending application or petition.

USCIS Privacy Act Statement

AUTHORITIES: The information requested on this form is collected pursuant to section 103(a) of the Immigration and Nationality Act, as amended INA section 101, et seq.

PURPOSE: The primary purpose for providing the information on this form is to request an electronic notification when USCIS accepts immigration form. The information you provide will be used to send you a text and/or email message.

DISCLOSURE: The information you provide is voluntary. However, failure to provide the requested information may prevent USCIS from providing you a text and/or email message receipting your immigration form.

ROUTINE USES: The information provided on this form will be used by and disclosed to DHS personnel and contractors in accordance with approved routine uses, as described in the associated published system of records notices [DHS/USCIS-007 - Benefits Information System and DHS/USCIS-001 - Alien File (A-File) and Central Index System (CIS), which can be found at www.dhs.gov/privacy]. The information may also be made available, as appropriate for law enforcement purposes or in the interest of national security.

Complete this form and clip it on top of the first page of your immigration form(s).

Applicant/Petitioner Full Last Name	Applicant/Petitioner Full First Name	Applicant/Petitioner Full Middle Name
▮	▮	▮

Email Address		Mobile Phone Number (Text Message)
▮		▮

FORM N-600:

Application for Certificate of Citizenship

OMB No. 1615-0057; Expires 12/31/2014

Department of Homeland Security
U. S. Citizenship and Immigration Services

Form N-600, Application for Certificate of Citizenship

Print or type all your answers fully and accurately in black ink. Write or type "N/A" if an item is not applicable. Write or type "None" if the answer is none. Failure to answer all of the questions may delay processing your Form N-600.

Part 1. Information About Your Eligibility (*Check only one box. USCIS will reject your Form N-600 if you check more than one box.*)	Your A-Number *if any:* A ▉▉▉▉▉▉▉

This application is being filed based on the fact that:

1. ☒ I am a BIOLOGICAL child of a U.S. citizen parent(s).

2. ☐ I am an ADOPTED child of a U.S. citizen parent(s).

3. ☐ Other *(explain fully)*:

Bar Code	Date Stamp
	Remarks
Action	

Part 2. Information About You (*Provide information about yourself if you are a person applying for the Certificate of Citizenship.* **Provide information about your child** *if you are a U.S. citizen parent applying for a Certificate of Citizenship for your minor child.*)

1. **Current Legal Name** *(do not provide a nickname)*

Family Name *(last name)*
▉▉▉▉▉▉▉▉▉▉

Given Name *(first name)*   Middle Name *(if applicable)*
▉▉▉▉▉

2. **Your name exactly as it appears on your Permanent Resident Card** *(if different from above)*

Family Name *(last name)*

Given Name *(first name)*   Middle Name *(if applicable)*

3. Other name(s) you have used since birth *(if applicable. Include nicknames)*

Family Name *(last name)*	Given Name *(first name)*	Middle Name *(if applicable)*

4. **U.S. Social Security Number** *(if applicable)*	5. **Date of Birth** *(mm/dd/yyyy)*	6. **Country of Birth**
N/A	05/23/1983	MEXICO

7. **Country of Prior Citizenship/Nationality**

   USA

8. **Gender**   ☒ Male   ☐ Female

9. **Height**   Feet 5   Inches 10

10. **Home Address**

    Street Number and Name *(do **not** provide a P.O. Box in this space unless it is your **ONLY** address)*   Apartment Number

    ████████████   A

City	State	Zip Code
AZUSA		

Province *(foreign address only)*	Country *(foreign address only)*	Postal Code *(foreign address only)*

11. **Mailing Address**

    C/O *(in care of name, if applicable)*

    Street Number and Name   Apartment Number

    ████████████   A

City	State	Zip Code
AZUSA		

Province *(foreign address only)*	Country *(foreign address only)*	Postal Code *(foreign address only)*

12. **Daytime Phone Number**   **Work Phone Number** *(if any)*   **Evening Phone Number**

    (██████████   ██████████3

    Mobile Phone Number *(if any)*   13. **E-Mail Address** *(if any)*

    (███████████   ████████████████

14. **Current Marital Status**

    ☐ Single, Never Married   ☒ Married   ☐ Divorced   ☐ Widowed

    ☐ Marriage Annulled   ☐ Other *(explain)*: _____

15. Are you a member or veteran of any branch of the U.S. Armed Forces?   ☐ Yes   ☒ No

16. **Information about admission into the United States and current immigration status**

    A. I arrived in the following manner

Port of Entry *(City/State)*	Date of Entry *(mm/dd/yyyy)*	Exact Name Used at Time of Entry:
ANDRADE, CA	04/15/1997	████████████████

    B. I used the following travel document to be admitted to the United States

    ☐ Passport   Passport Number   Passport Issuing Country   Date Passport Issued *(mm/dd/yyyy)*

    ☒ Other *(specify document name and issuance date(s))*

    WAIVED THROUGH

C. I am

☐ A Permanent Resident

☐ A Nonimmigrant

☐ A Refugee/Asylee

☒ Other *(explain)*   **USC (DERIVATIVE)**

D. I obtained permanent resident status through adjustment of status in the United States or admission as a permanent resident *(if applicable)*

Date I became a permanent resident *(mm/dd/yyyy)*	USCIS office that granted my permanent resident status or location where I was admitted
N/A	N/A

17. Have you previously applied for a Certificate of Citizenship or U.S. passport? ☒ Yes *(attach explanation)* ☐ No

18. Have you ever abandoned or lost your permanent resident status? ☐ Yes *(attach explanation)* ☒ No

19. Were you adopted? ☐ Yes *(complete the following information)* ☒ No

Date of Adoption *(mm/dd/yyyy)*	Place of Final Adoption *(City/State or Country)*

Date Legal Custody Began *(mm/dd/yyyy)*	Date Physical Custody Began *(mm/dd/yyyy)*

20. Did you have to be re-adopted in the United States? ☐ Yes *(complete the following information)* ☒ No

Date of Final Adoption *(mm/dd/yyyy)*	Place of Final Adoption *(City/State)*

Date Legal Custody Began *(mm/dd/yyyy)*	Date Physical Custody Began *(mm/dd/yyyy)*

21. Were your parents married to each other when you were born (or adopted)? ☐ Yes ☒ No

22. Did your parents marry after you were born? ☐ Yes ☒ No

23. Do you regularly reside in the United States in the legal and physical custody of your U.S. citizen parent(s)? ☒ Yes ☐ No

24. Have you been absent from the United States since you first arrived? ☒ Yes ☐ No

*(complete the following information **only if you are claiming U.S. citizenship at the time of birth if you were born before October 10, 1952**)*

Date You Left the United States *(mm/dd/yyyy)*	Date You Returned to the United States *(mm/dd/yyyy)*	Place of Entry Upon Return to the United States *(City, State)*

Part 3. Information About Your U.S. Citizen Biological Father (or Adoptive Father) (*Complete this section if you are claiming citizenship through a U.S. citizen biological father (or adoptive father).* ***Provide information about yourself*** *if you are a U.S. citizen father applying for a Certificate of Citizenship on behalf of your minor biological or adopted child.*)

A ███████████

1. **Current legal name of U.S. citizen father**

Family Name *(last name)*	Given Name *(first name)*	Middle Name *(if applicable)*
███████████	███████████	████████

2. **Date of Birth** *(mm/dd/yyyy)*
   07/16/1955

3. **Country of Birth**
   MEXICO

4. **Country of Citizenship/Nationality**
   MEXICO

5. **Home Address**

Street Number and Name *(write "Deceased" and date of death if your father has passed away)* ███████████ — Apartment Number

City	State	Zip Code
YUMA		

Province *(foreign address only)*	Country *(foreign address only)*	Postal Code *(foreign address only)*

6. **My father is a U.S. citizen by**

   [ ] Birth in the United States
   [ ] Acquisition after birth through naturalization of alien parent(s)
   [ ] Birth abroad to U.S. citizen parent(s)

   Certificate of Citizenship Number — A-Number *(if known)*

   [X] Naturalization

   Date of Naturalization *(mm/dd/yyyy)* — Place of Naturalization *(name of court and City/State or USCIS office location)*

   Certificate of Naturalization Number — A-Number *(if known)*

7. **Has your father ever lost U.S. citizenship or taken any action that would cause loss of U.S. citizenship?**

   [ ] Yes *(provide full explanation on an additional sheet(s) of paper)*   [X] No

8. **Marital History**

   A. How many times has your U.S. citizen father been married *(including annulled marriages and marriage(s) to the same person)*? **1**

   B. What is your U.S. citizen father's current marital status?

   [ ] Single, Never Married   [ ] Married   [ ] Separated   [X] Divorced   [ ] Widowed

   [ ] Marriage Annulled   [ ] Other *(explain)*: _____

Part 3. Information About Your U.S. Citizen Biological Father (or Adoptive Father) *(Continued)*

A [redacted]

C. Information about U.S. citizen father's current spouse

Family Name *(last name)*

Given Name *(first name)*

Middle Name *(if applicable)*

Date of Birth *(mm/dd/yyyy)*

Country of Birth

Country of Citizenship/Nationality

Spouse's Home Address

Street Number and Name

Apartment Number

City

State

Zip Code

Province *(foreign address only)*

Country *(foreign address only)*

Postal Code *(foreign address only)*

Date of Marriage *(mm/dd/yyyy)*

Place of Marriage *(City/State or Country)*

Spouse's Immigration Status

☐ U.S. Citizen   ☐ Permanent Resident   ☐ Other *(explain)*: _____

D. Is your U.S. citizen father's current spouse also your biological (or adopted) mother?   ☐ Yes   ☒ No

Part 4. Information About Your U.S. Citizen Biological Mother (or Adoptive Mother) *(Complete this section if you are claiming citizenship through a U.S. citizen biological mother (or adoptive mother). Provide information about yourself if you are a U.S. citizen mother applying for a Certificate of Citizenship on behalf of your minor biological or adopted child.)*

1. **Current legal name of U.S. citizen mother**

Family Name *(last name)*

Given Name *(first name)*

Middle Name *(if applicable)*

2. **Date of Birth** *(mm/dd/yyyy)*

3. **Country of Birth**

4. **Country of Citizenship/Nationality**

5. **Home Address**

Street Number and Name *(write "Deceased" and date of death if your mother has passed away)*

Apartment Number

City

State

Zip Code

Province *(foreign address only)*

Country *(foreign address only)*

Postal Code *(foreign address only)*

6. **My mother is a U.S. citizen by**

☐ Birth in the United States

☐ Acquisition after birth through naturalization of alien parent(s)

☐ Birth abroad to U.S. citizen parent(s)

Certificate of Citizenship Number	A-Number *(if known)*

☐ Naturalization

Date of Naturalization *(mm/dd/yyyy)*	Place of Naturalization *(name of court and City/State or USCIS office location)*

Certificate of Naturalization Number	A-Number *(if known)*

7. **Has your mother ever lost U.S. citizenship or taken any action that would cause loss of U.S. citizenship?**

☐ Yes *(provide full explanation on an additional sheet(s) of paper)*   ☐ No

8. **Marital History**

A. How many times has your U.S. citizen mother been married *(including annulled marriages and marriage(s) to the same person)*? _____

B. What is your U.S. citizen mother's current marital status?

☐ Single, Never Married   ☐ Married   ☐ Separated   ☐ Divorced   ☐ Widowed

☐ Marriage Annulled   ☐ Other *(explain)*: _____

C. Information about U.S. citizen mother's current spouse

Family Name *(last name)*	Given Name *(first name)*	Middle Name *(if applicable)*

Date of Birth *(mm/dd/yyyy)*	Country of Birth	Country of Citizenship/Nationality

Spouse's Home Address

Street Number and Name	Apartment Number

City	State	Zip Code

Province *(foreign address only)*	Country *(foreign address only)*	Postal Code *(foreign address only)*

Date of Marriage *(mm/dd/yyyy)*	Place of Marriage *(City/State or Country)*

Spouse's Immigration Status

☐ U.S. Citizen   ☐ Permanent Resident   ☐ Other *(explain)*: _____

D. Is your U.S. citizen mother's current spouse also your biological (or adopted) father?   ☐ Yes   ☐ No

Part 5. Physical Presence in the United States From Birth Until Filing of Form N-600 (*Only applicants born outside the United States claiming to have been born U.S. citizens are required to provide all the dates when your U.S. citizen biological father or U.S. citizen biological mother resided in the United States. **Include all dates from your birth until the date you file your Form N-600.**)*

A ▮▮▮▮▮▮▮

Indicate whether this information relates to your U.S. citizen (USC) father or mother

☒ USC Father   ☐ USC Mother

Physical Presence in the United States *(mm/dd/yyyy)*							
From	07/01/1971	Until	07/22/1971	From		Until	
From	01/01/1972	Until		From		Until	
From	12/01/1972	Until	12/22/1972	From		Until	
From	06/22/1973	Until	02/25/2014	From		Until	

Part 6. Information About Military Service of U. S. Citizen Parent(s) *(Complete this only if you are an applicant claiming U.S. citizenship at time of birth abroad.)*

1. Has your U.S. citizen parent(s) served in the U.S. Armed Forces?   ☐ Yes   ☒ No

2. If "Yes," which parent?   ☐ U.S. Citizen Father   ☐ U.S. Citizen Mother

3. Dates of Service *(if time of service fulfills any of required physical presence, submit evidence of service)*

From *(mm/dd/yyyy)*   To *(mm/dd/yyyy)*   From *(mm/dd/yyyy)*   To *(mm/dd/yyyy)*

4. Type of discharge   ☐ Honorable   ☐ Other than Honorable   ☐ Dishonorable

Part 7. Your Signature *(USCIS will reject your Form N-600 if it is not signed.)*

I certify, under penalty of perjury under the laws of the United States, that this application and the evidence submitted with it is all true and correct. I authorize the release of any information from my records, or my minor child's records, that U.S. Citizenship and Immigration Services needs to determine eligibility for the benefit I am seeking.

Your Signature *(parent may sign on behalf of a minor child)*

▮▮▮▮▮▮▮▮▮▮▮▮▮▮R

Date *(mm/dd/yyyy)*
02/25/2014

Part 8. Signature of Person Who Prepared This Form N-600 For You *(if applicable)*

I declare that I prepared this application at the request of the above person. The answers provided are based on information of which I have personal knowledge and/or were provided to me by the above-named person in response to the questions contained on this form.

Preparer's Printed Name
BRIAN D. LERNER

Preparer's Signature

Date *(mm/dd/yyyy)*
02/25/2014

Part 8. Signature of Person Who Prepared This Form N-600 For You *(if applicable)*

| | A | 200-047-267 |

Preparer's Firm or Organization Name *(if applicable)*

LAW OFFICES OF BRIAN D. LERNER, APC

Preparer's Daytime Phone Number

(562) 495-0554

Preparer's Address

Street Number and Name

3233 E. BROADWAY

City	State	Zip Code
LONG BEACH		

Province *(foreign address only)*	Country *(foreign address only)*	Postal Code *(foreign address only)*

Preparer's E-Mail Address

BLERNER@CALIFORNIAIMMIGRATION.US

Preparer's Fax Number

(562) 608-8672

NOTE: Do not complete the next part unless the USCIS officer instructs you to do so at the interview.

I, the (applicant, parent, or legal guardian) _____ do swear or affirm, under penalty of perjury under the laws of the United States, that I know and understand the contents of this application signed by me, and the attached supplementary pages number (___) to (___) inclusive, that the same are true and correct to the best of my knowledge, and that corrections number (___) to (___) were made by me or at my request.

Applicant's, Parent's, or Legal Guardian's Signature   **Date** *(mm/dd/yyyy)*

Subscribed and sworn or affirmed before me upon examination of the applicant (parent, legal guardian) on _____ at
                                                                                                    (mm/dd/yyyy)
_____ .
                    (Location)

USCIS Officer's Name and Title   **USCIS Officer's Signature**

Part 10. Officer Report and Recommendation on Application for Certificate of Citizenship *(for USCIS use ONLY)*

On the basis of the documents, records, the testimony of person(s) examined, and the identification upon personal appearance of the underage beneficiary, I find that all the facts and conclusions set forth under oath in this application are:

1. ☐ True and correct

2. ☐ The applicant derived or acquired U.S. citizenship on _____
                                                                    (mm/dd/yyyy)

3. ☐ The applicant derived or acquired U.S. citizenship through *(mark "X" next to the appropriate section of law, or if the section of law is not reflected, write the applicable section of law in the space next to "Other")*
    ☐ *Section 301 of the INA*
    ☐ *Section 309 of the INA*
    ☐ *Section 320 of the INA*
    ☐ *Section 321 of the INA*
    ☐ *Other:* _____

4. ☐ The applicant has not been expatriated since that time

I recommend that this Form N-600 application be   ☐ Approved   ☐ Denied

Issue Certificate of Citizenship in the name of

Last Name	First Name	Middle Name

USCIS Officer's Name and Title   **USCIS Officer's Signature**   **Date** *(mm/dd/yyyy)*

I do _____ do not _____ concur with the USCIS Officer's recommendation of the Form N-600.

USCIS District Director's or Field Office Director's Signature   **Date** *(mm/dd/yyyy)*

EXHIBITS

Applicant's Birth Certificate with English Translation

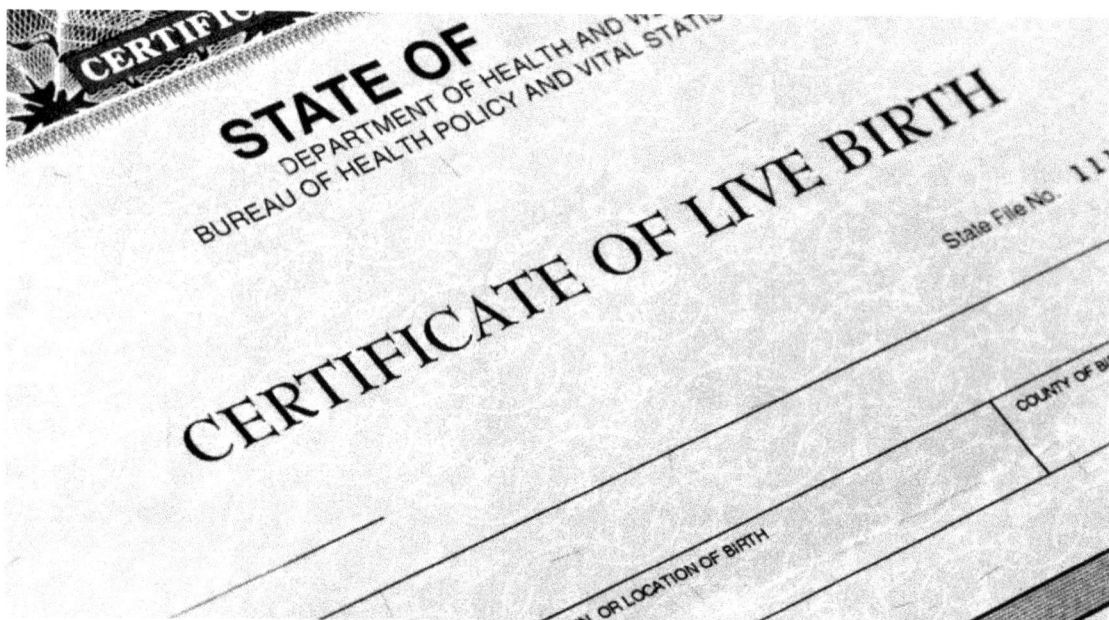

ESTADOS UNIDOS MEXICANOS
GOBIERNO DEL ESTADO
LIBRE Y SOBERANO
DE BAJA CALIFORNIA
REGISTRO CIVIL

A1-28-017

No. DE CONTROL Nº 35280

ACTA DE NACIMIENTO

CLAVE UNICA DE REG. DE POBLACION

020020183078892

OFICIALIA No.	LIBRO No.	ACTA No.	LOCALIDAD	FECHA DE REGISTRO		
				DIA	MES	AÑO
001	1	73	LOS ALGODONES			
MUNICIPIO O DELEGACION			ENTIDAD FEDERATIVA			
		MEXICALI	BAJA CALIFORNIA	12	07	83

REGISTRADO   SEXO: MASCULINO ⊗   FEMENINO ○

NOMBRE _____   PRIMER APELLIDO _____   SEGUNDO APELLIDO _____

FECHA DE NACIMIENTO ___ 23 DE MAYO DE 1983 ___

LUGAR DE NACIMIENTO ___ LOS ALGODONES, MEXICALI BAJA CALIFORNIA ___

PADRES

NOMBRE DEL PADRE _____   NACIONALIDAD MEXICANA

DOMICILIO ___ YUMA ARIZONA, E. U. A. ___   ORIGEN CD. MORELOS, B.C.

NOMBRE DE LA MADRE _____   NACIONALIDAD MEXICANA

DOMICILIO ___ LOS ALGODONES, BAJA CALIFORNIA ___   ORIGEN LOS ALGODONES, B.C.

ABUELOS

ABUELO PATERNO _____   NACIONALIDAD NORTE AMERICANA

ABUELA PATERNA ___ ALICIA MENA POMPA. ___   NACIONALIDAD MEXICANA

DOMICILIO ___ YUMA ARIZONA, E. U. A. ___

ABUELO MATERNO _____   NACIONALIDAD MEXICANA

ABUELA MATERNA _____   NACIONALIDAD MEXICANA

DOMICILIO ___ LOS ALGODONES, BAJA CALIF. ___

TESTIGOS

NOMBRE _____   NACIONALIDAD MEXICANA

DOMICILIO ___ CALLEJON ALAMO No.185 LOS ALGODONES, B.C. ___

NOMBRE _____   NACIONALIDAD MEXICANA

DOMICILIO ___ LOS ALGODONES, BAJA CALIFORNIA ___

SE DIO LECTURA A LA PRESENTE ACTA Y CONFORMES CON SU CONTENIDO LA
RATIFICARON Y FIRMARON QUIENES EN ELLA INTERVINIERON Y SABEN HACERLO.

ES COPIA FIEL EXACTA DE SU ORIGINAL QUE SE COMPULSA Y AUTORIZA CON MI FIRMA
Y SELLO DE ESTA OFICINA A SOLICITUD DE PARTE INTERESADA Y CERTIFICO EN LA
CIUDAD ___ DE LOS ALGODONES, ___ BAJA CALIFORNIA, A
___ 29 ___ DE ___ JUNIO ___ DE 2004

NOMBRE

EL OFICIAL DEL REGISTRO CIVIL

mazt.

BIRTHCERTIFICATE NO. 73 _____

BIRTH OF ____ ███████████████████████ ____

DATE OF BIRTH ___ May 23, 1983 _____

PLACE OF BIRTH ___ LOS ALGODONES,B.C. MEX. ____

PARENTS

NAME ___ ██████████████████ ·   NAME ___ ██████████████████

AGE _____ UNKNOWN _____   AGE ___ UNKNOWN _____

NATIONALITY___ AMERICAN _____   NATION. ___ MEXCAN _____

STATUS ___ UNKNOWN _____   STATUS ___ UNKNOWN _____

ADRESS _YUMA,AZ. U.S.A. _____   ADRESS _LOS ALGODONES,B.C._

OCCUPATION ___ UNKNOWN _____   OCCUPATION ___ UNKNOWN ____

FATHER'S PARENTS

NAME ███████████████████ ___   NAME ___ ███████████████.

ADDRESS ___ YUMA,AZ. U.S.A. _____   ADRESS _YUMA,AZ. U.S.A. ___

MOTHER'S PARENTS

NAME ___ █████████████████ __   NAME __ ████████████████ _

ADDRESS _LOS ALGODONES,B.C._____   ADDRESS _LOS ALGODONES,B.C.

WITNESSES

NAME _/███████████████████   NAME ___ ███████████████

ADDRESS _CALLEJON ALAMO 185 _____   ADDRESS _LOS ALGODONES,B.C._
        LOS ALGODONES,B.C.

THIS IS A TRANSLATION OF AN ORIGINAL BIRTHCERTIFICATE FROM SPANISH

SIGN THIS _3rd_ DAY OF _OCTOBER_ OF19_91_.

NOTARY PUBLIC _____ _(signature)_ _____
MY EXPIRATION DATE IS ___ 05-07-97 _____ .

Applicant's Identification Card

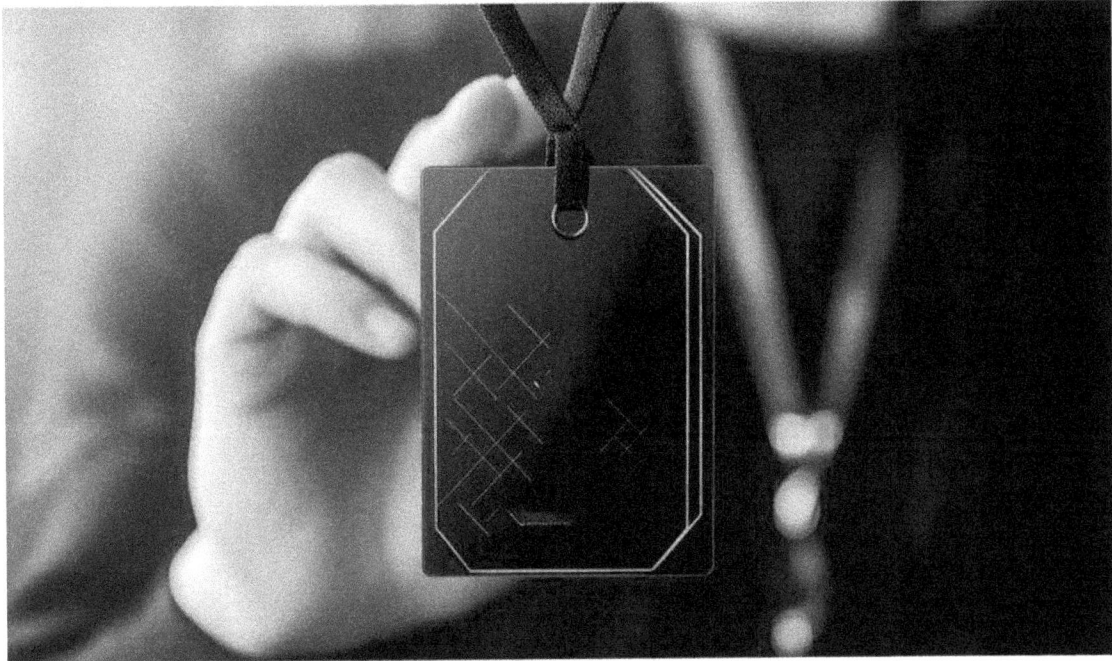

MEXICO MATRICULA CONSULAR CONSULAR ID CARD

Nombre/Name

Lugar y Fecha de Nacimiento/Place of Birth and Birth Date
MEXICALI
B.C., MEX. 23 MAY 1983

Dirección/Address

Fecha de Emisión/Date of Issue
15 FEB 2012

Fecha de Expiración/Date of Expiry
15 FEB 2017

Autoridad/Authority
CONSULMEX
MOVIL LOS ANGELES   10039425

10039425

:<<<<<
:<<<<5
:<<<<<

EXHIBIT '3'

Father's Certificate of Naturalization

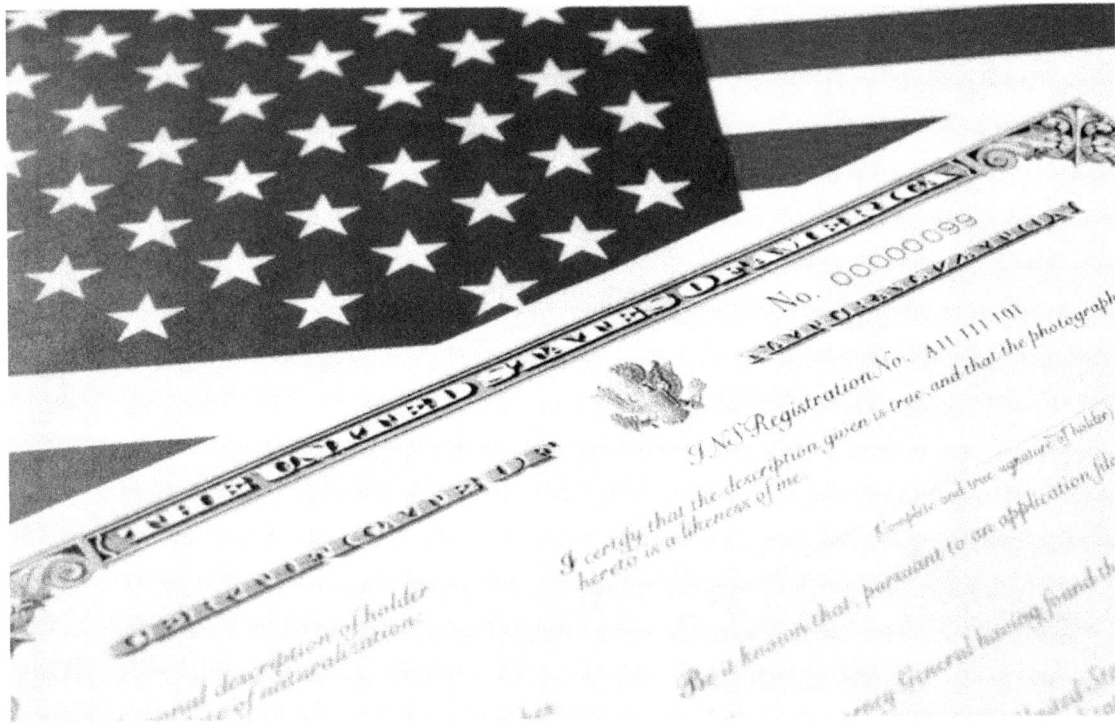

UNITED STATES OF AMERICA

CERTIFICATE OF NATURALIZATION

No. 1189 5122

U.S. Registration No. ___

FORM N-570 (REV. 11-1-87)

845022

DEPARTMENT OF JUSTICE

Personal description of holder as of date of naturalization: Date of birth JULY 16, 1955 ; sex MALE ;
complexion MEDIUM ; color of eyes ___ ; color of hair ___ ; height 5 feet 09 inches ;
weight _____ pounds; visible distinctive marks ___
Marital status DIVORCED ; Country of former nationality MEXICO

(Complete and true signature of holder)

Seal

Be it known that, ___ residing at YUMA, ARIZONA
having applied to the Commissioner of Immigration and Naturalization for a Certificate
of Naturalization and having found that the petitioner is entitled to be admitted a citizen of the United States of America
WAS NATURALIZED BY THE UNITED STATES DISTRICT COURT FOR
THE DISTRICT OF ARIZONA AT PHOENIX, ARIZONA ON APRIL 30,
1983.

Now therefore, in pursuance of the authority contained in Section 310(a)
of the Immigration and Nationality Act, this Certificate of Naturalization is
issued this TENTH day of MAY
TWO-THOUSAND FOUR
and the seal of the Department of Justice affixed pursuant to statute.

COMMISSIONER OF IMMIGRATION AND NATURALIZATION

EXHIBIT '4'

Father's Declaration

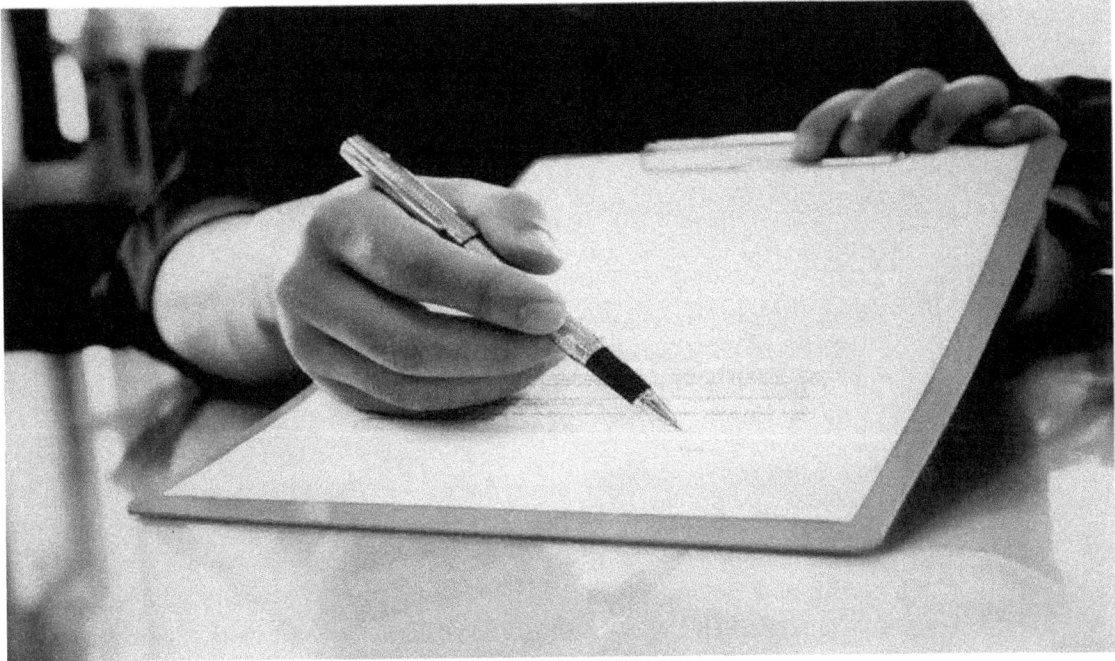

████████████

YUMA, AZ 85364

████████████

To whom it may concern:

My name is ████████████ I was born on July 16, 1955 in Ejido Tabasco, Baja California, Mexico. I am U.S. Naturalized citizen.

I am ████████████ father. Since my son ████████ was born I took care of him. He came to live with me in 1997. I enrolled him in Crane middle school in Yuma, Arizona and he graduated from Yuma High School. I was in charge of providing food, clothing, shelter and his basic needs. I would go to his school conferences and would meet with his teachers. At that time we lived at ████████ ████████████, Yuma, Arizona.

My son, ████████, is a very caring, responsible and lovable person. All this time I have never had any problems with him. My son ████████ has two U.S. citizen children, ████████████████████ is five years old and ████████ is nine months old.

Thank you for your attention to this matter.

Dated this __11__ day of July, 2013.

[signature]

████████████

STATE OF ARIZONA   )
) SS.
County of Yuma   )

SUBSCRIBED AND SWORN to before me this ____ day of July, 2013, by Francisco Montoya.

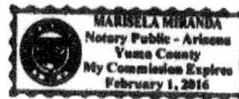

NOTARY PUBLIC

My commission expires:

Feb. 1, 2016

Proof of Support Provided by Father to Applicant as Evidence of Paternity

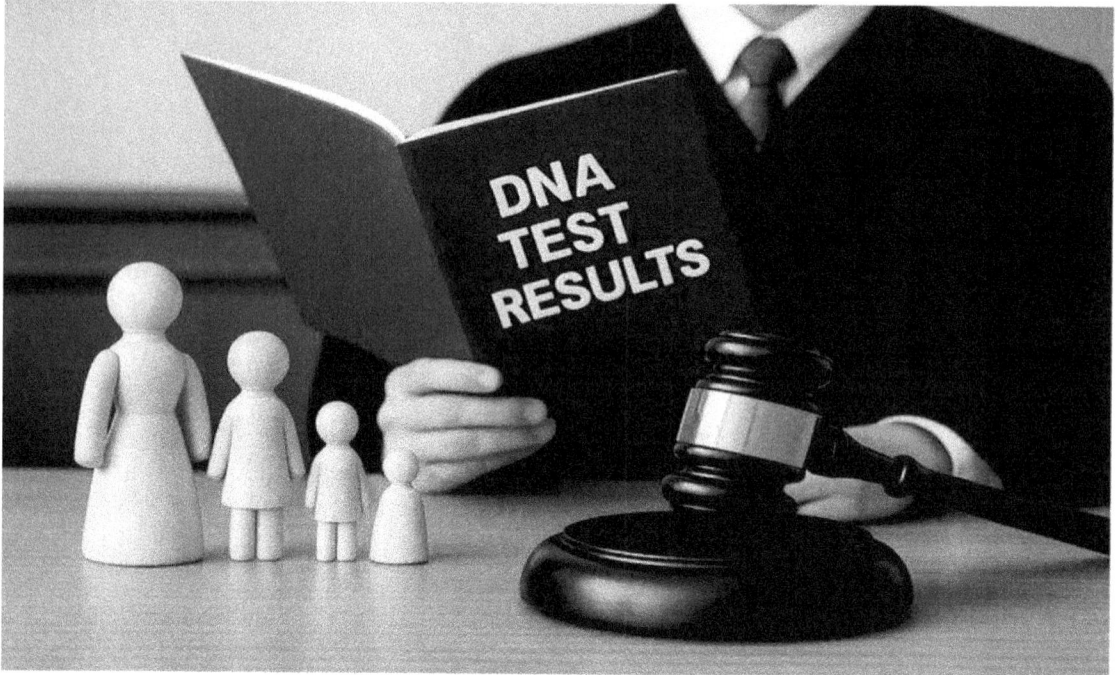

SUMMARY FICA EARNINGS FOR YEARS REQUESTED

YEAR	EARNINGS	YEAR	EARNINGS	YEAR	EARNINGS	YEAR	EARNINGS
1973	313.60	1983	4022.63	1992	5763.26	2001	.00
1974	4557.84	1984	2495.14	1993	.00	2002	.00
1975	5324.95	1985	1722.39	1994	.00	2003	6456.37
1976	4292.41	1986	2168.00	1995	.00	2004	10324.72
1977	2250.06	1987	.00	1996	.00	2005	8874.08
1978	10395.27	1988	935.02	1997	120.00	2006	8614.67
1979	19512.57	1989	1949.05	1998	5490.20	2007	1529.10
1980	23587.91	1990	2090.00	1999	2598.75	2008	5939.82
1981	14468.80	1991	6146.00	2000	.00	2009	4364.58
1982	14780.33						

SUMMARY MQGE EARNINGS FOR YEARS REQUESTED
NO MQGE EARNINGS FOR YEARS REQUESTED

REMARKS
NON-COVERED EARNINGS PRESENT FOR: 2003-2007

Social Security Administration
1235 So. Redondo Center Drive
Yuma, AZ 85365

Photos Showing Relationship of Applicant and His Father

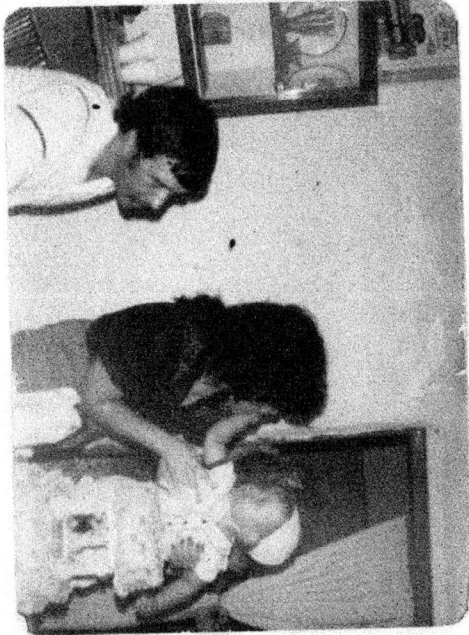

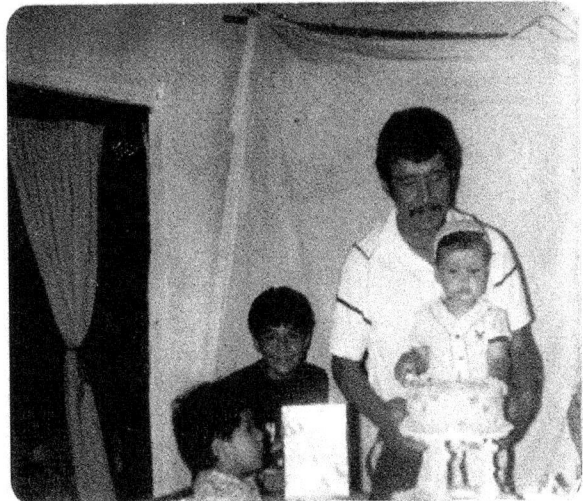

Mother's Death Certificate with English Translation

DEPARTMENT OF HEALTH AND WELFARE
BUREAU OF VITAL RECORDS AND HEALTH STATISTICS

CERTIFICATE OF DEATH

ESTADOS UNIDOS MEXICANOS
GOBIERNO DEL ESTADO
LIBRE Y SOBERANO
DE BAJA CALIFORNIA
REGISTRO CIVIL

No. DE CONTROL **0032**

ACTA DE DEFUNCION

CLAVE DE REGISTRO E IDENTIFICACION (CRIP)

OFICIALIA No.	LIBRO No.	ACTA No.	LOCALIDAD	FECHA DE REGISTRO
04-09	1,	0032,	LOS ALGODONES	DIA 24 MES 12 AÑO 2003

MUNICIPIO MEXICALI — MEXICALI — **ENTIDAD FEDERATIVA** BAJA CALIFORNIA

SEXO MASCULINO ○ FEMENINO ☒

NOMBRE (NOMBRE S) (PRIMER APELLIDO) (SEGUNDO APELLIDO) ▉

EDO. CIVIL VIUDA **NACIONALIDAD** MEXICANA **EDAD** AÑOS 45 MESES 07 DIAS HORAS **FECHA DE NACIMIENTO** 31 DE MAYO DE 1958

DOMICILIO HABITUAL AV. *B* #696
LOS ALGODONES — MEXICALI — BAJA CALIFORNIA — MEXICO
LOCALIDAD — MUNICIPIO — ENTIDAD — PAIS

LUGAR DE NACIMIENTO LOS ALGODONES, MEXICALI, BAJA CALIFORNIA — MEXICO
LOCALIDAD — MUNICIPIO — ENTIDAD — PAIS

NOMBRE DEL CONYUGE ▉ **NACIONALIDAD** ▉

NOMBRE DEL PADRE: ▉

NOMBRE DE LA MADRE: ▉

FALLECIMIENTO

FECHA DE DEFUNCION 22 DE DICIEMBRE DEL 2003 **HORA** 21:15 HRS.

LUGAR CALLE DEL HOSPITAL S/N CENTRO CIVICO MEXICALI **CLAVE** 040004368

DESTINO DEL CADAVER INHUMACION ○ **CREMACION** ○ **NOMBRE DEL PANTEON O CREMATORIO** EJIDO CULIACAN

UBICACION EJIDO CULIACAN, LOS ALGODONES, B.C. **ORDEN No.** 00037

DONDE FALLECIO CALLE DEL HOSPITAL S/N CENTRO CIVICO MEXICALI, B.C.

CAUSA(S) DE LA MUERTE INSUF. RESPIRATORIA, ACIDOSIS METABOLICA, INSUF. RENAL AGUDA, CANCER CERVICO UTERINO III ETAPAS

TIPO DE DEFUNCION ENFERMEDAD

NOMBRE DEL MEDICO QUE CERTIFICO LA DEFUNCION RICARDO GAROTA AUDELO

No. DE CEDULA PROFESIONAL 1167347

DOMICILIO REFORMA 1533 CENTRO MEXICALI, B.C.

DECLARANTE

NOMBRE ▉ **EDAD** 32 AÑOS

NACIONALIDAD MEXICANA **PARENTESCO** HERMANO DE LA FALLECIDA

DOMICILIO AV. *A* #235 LOS ALGODONES, B.C. **OCUPACION** AGRICULTOR

TESTIGOS

NOMBRE ▉ **NACIONALIDAD** MEXICANA **EDAD** 27 AÑOS

DOMICILIO LOS ALGODONES, B.C. **OCUPACION** COMERCIANTE **PARENTESCO** NINGUNO

NOMBRE EMILY SIBAJA MAZARIEGOS **NACIONALIDAD** MEXICANA **EDAD** 33 AÑOS

DOMICILIO LOS ALGODONES, B.C. **OCUPACION** EMPLEADO **PARENTESCO** NINGUNO

LA PRESENTE ACTA TIENE ANEXAS LAS ANOTACIONES SIGUIENTES:

FIRMAS

DECLARANTE — TESTIGO — TESTIGO

M. DEL ALVARDO SOTO
TESTIGO

SE DIO LECTURA A LA PRESENTE ACTA Y CONFORME CON SU CONTENIDO LA RATIFICAN Y FIRMAN QUIENES EN ELLA INTERVINIERON, SABEN HACERLO Y QUIENES NO IMPRIMEN SU HUELLA DIGITAL DOY FE.

SELLO DE LA OFICIALIA DEL REGISTRO CIVIL

OFICIALIA No. 04-09 DE BAJA CALIFORNIA

C. ▉

OFICIAL

MXL 0354212

37

A1-28-19

No de Control:

ESTADOS UNIDOS MEXICANOS   Nº 8684
Estado Libre y Soberano de Baja California

REGISTRO CIVIL

En nombre del Estado Libre y Soberano de Baja California y como Oficial __01__ del Registro Civil de
este Municipio, CERTIFICO: Que en el Libro No. __1__ del Registro Civil que es a mi cargo, en la Foja
No. __0032__ se encuentra el Acta No. __0032__ de fecha 24 DE DICIEMBRE DEL 2003
levantada por el C. JORGE MARIO COCHRAN MONGE. OFICIAL
del Registro Civil DE LOS ALGODONES, B.C. en la cual se contienen los siguientes datos:

ACTA DE DEFUNCION

FINADO   Sexo: Masculino ( )   Femenino XXX

Nombre: ███████████

Estado Civil: VIUDA.   Nacionalidad: MEXICANA   Edad: 45 Años

Domicilio: ███████████

Nombre del Cónyuge: - - - - - - - -   Nacionalidad: MEXICANA

Nombre del Padre: ███████████

Nombre de la Madre: ███████████

FALLECIMIENTO

Destino del Cadáver: Inhumación (X) Cremación ( ) Nombre del panteón o Crematorio: EJIDO CULIACAN
Ubicación EJIDO CULIACAN LOS ALGODONES, B.C.   Orden No. 00037
Fecha de la Defunción: 22 DE DICIEMBRE DEL 2003
Lugar: CALLE DEL HOSPITAL S/N CENTRO CIVICO MEXICALI, B.C.
Causa(s) de la Muerte: INSUF. RESPIRATORIA, ACIDOSIS METABOLICA, INSUF. RENAL AGUDA
CANCER CERVICO UTERINO III, 5 MESES.

Nombre del Médico que Certificó la Defunción	No. de Cédula Profesional
RICARDO GARCIA AUDELO.	1167347

Domicilio: REFORMA 1533 CENTRO MEXICALI, B.C.

DECLARANTES

Nombre: ███████████   Edad: 32 Años
Nacionalidad: MEXICANA   Parentesco: ███████████
Domicilio: AV. "A" # 235 LOS ALGODONES, B.C.

TESTIGOS

Nombre: ███████████   Edad: 27 Años
Nacionalidad: MEXICANA   Parentesco: NINGUNO
Domicilio: LOS ALGODONES, B.C.
Nombre: ███████████   Edad: 33 Años
Nacionalidad: MEXICANA   Parentesco: NINGUNO
Domicilio: LOS ALGODONES, B.C.

FIRMAS

███████████

DECLARANTE

███████████

TESTIGO   TESTIGO

Copy of High School Diploma

Yuma High School

Yuma   Arizona

This Certifies That

has satisfactorily completed the Course of Studies prescribed for graduation from this high school and is therefore awarded this

Diploma

Given this twenty-fourth day of May, two thousand and two.

SUPERINTENDENT, YUMA UNION HIGH SCHOOL DISTRICT

PRESIDENT, YUMA UNION HIGH SCHOOL DISTRICT BOARD OF EDUCATION

PRINCIPAL, YUMA HIGH SCHOOL

ASSISTANT PRINCIPAL, ACADEMICS

EXHIBIT '9'

Copy of Authorization to Act as a Solo Parent

AUTHORIZATION TO ACT IN LOCO PARENTIS

I, ██████████████████ , BEING THE NATURAL PARENT OF
    (NAME OF NATURAL PARENT)
██████████████████ , BORN 05-23-83
(NAME OF MINOR CHILD)   (DATE OF BIRTH)

DO HEREBY DESIGNATE ██████████████████ ,
                          (DESIGNEE)

TO ACT IN LOCO PARENTIS FOR SAID MINOR CHILD SINCE 06-30 ,97.

BY THIS DESIGNATION, I SPECIFICALLY INTEND TO AUTHORIZE THE SAID

██████████████████ TO OBTAIN NECESARY MEDICAL TREATMENT,
(DESIGNEE)

DISCIPLINE THE SAID MINOR CHILD, TO SIGN ANY AND ALL DOCUMENTS

RELATING TO THE CARE, CUSTODY AND RESPONSABILITY FOR THE MINOR,

INCLUDING REGISTRATION FOR SCHOOL AND DO ALL THINGS THAT HE/SHE

IN HIS/HER DISCRETION BELIEVES TO BE NECESSARY TO INSURE THE

HEALTH, WELFARE AND HAPPINESS OF SAID CHILD.

WITNESS:

_____   JUNE 30,97
(NAME OF PARENT SIGNATURE)   (DATE)

STATE OF ___ARIZONA___)
) SS
COUNTY OF ___YUMA___   )

ON THIS 30 DAY OF ___JUNE___ , 19 97, PERSONALLY

APPEARED BEFORE ME THE ABOVE NAMED PETITIONER ██████████████████

WHO MADE OATH THAT HE/SHE HAD READ THE FOREGOING PETITION BY HER/HIS

SUBSCRIBED AND KNOWS THE CONTENTS THEREOF AND THE SAME IS TRUE OF

HER/HIS KNOWLEDGE, EXCEPT AS TO THOSE MATTERS THEREIN STATED TO BE ON

HER/HIS INFORMATION AND BELIEF AND AS TO THOSE MATTERS SHE/HE BELIEVES IT

TO BE TRUE.

NOTARY/PUBLI
COMMISSION EXP

"OFFICIAL SEAL"
Maria Luisa Salcido
Notary Public-Arizona
Yuma County
My Commission Expires 9/27/97

EXHIBIT '10'

Copy of High School Student Registration

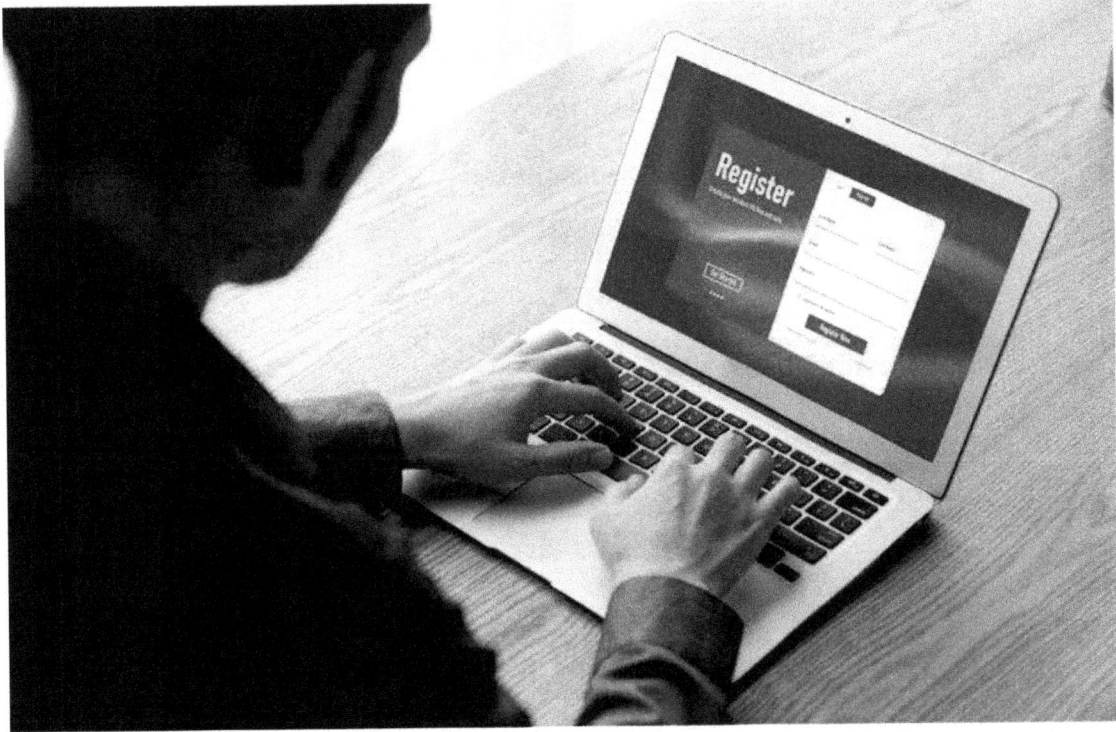

YUMA UNION HIGH SCHOOL DISTRICT
STUDENT REGISTRATION

FOR OFFICE USE ONLY

Student ID #

3	0	0	0	7

PLEASE PRINT

Open Enrollment Form submitted to: ☐ CHS ☐ KHS ☐ YHS

School (Check one ☒)
☐ Cibola ☐ Vista
☐ Kofa ☒ Yuma

Ethnic (Check one ☒)
☐ White ☐ Am Indian
☐ Black ☐ Asian
☒ Hispanic ☐ Other

STUDENT NAME

Last ▪▪▪▪▪ / First ▪▪▪▪▪ / Middle ▪▪▪▪▪

Sex ☒ M ☐ F. Grade 9

▪▪▪▪▪ Street Address City Yuma Zip Code 85364 Date of Birth 5/23/83

3390 Mailing Address ▪▪▪▪▪ City Zip Code Home Phone # 376 050?

Primary - Adult Responsible
Relationship to Student: ☒ Father ☐ Stepfather ☐ Guardian
☐ Mother ☐ Stepmother ☐ Other

Area Work #

Secondary - Adult Responsible Area Work #

Father ▪▪▪▪▪ Mother:

Father's Employer: Mother's Employer:

Emergency Contact ▪▪▪▪▪ Phone # Emergency Contact Phone #

Please check (☒) Junior H.S. from which student graduated:
☒ Crane
☐ Fourth Avenue
☐ San Luis Middle School
☐ Gila Vista
☐ Somerton Middle School
☐ Woodard

☐ Yuma Lutheran
☐ Mt. Zion
☐ St. Francis
☐ Immaculate Conception
☐ In State
☐ Out of State
☐ Mexico

Please check (☒) last school student attended
☐ CHS ☐ VS
☐ KHS ☐ YHS
☐ YUHS Summer School
☐ VS Summer School
☐ Continuation School
☐ Other

Birthplace

Mexico. City
Baja california State/Country

Home Language (Check one ☒)
☐ English
☒ Spanish
☐ Other

HOME LANGUAGE SURVEY

A. Which language did your child first speak? español

B. What language does your child use most at home? mama papa

C. What language do you use most in speaking to your child? español

D. What language is used most by the adults at home? Lo mismo que todos

Counselor: Migrant: ☒ Yes ☐ No Student SS#:

Is student currently under long term expulsion/suspension from any school? ☐ Yes ☒ No
Has student ever been enrolled in a Special Education Program? ☐ Yes ☒ No (Optional) If yes, where?
Has student ever been enrolled in an ESL or Bilingual Program? ☐ Yes ☒ No If yes, where?

X _Brenesa Winter_ Signature - Parent/Guardian/Responsible Person 1/12/98 Date

ABOUT THE AUTHOR

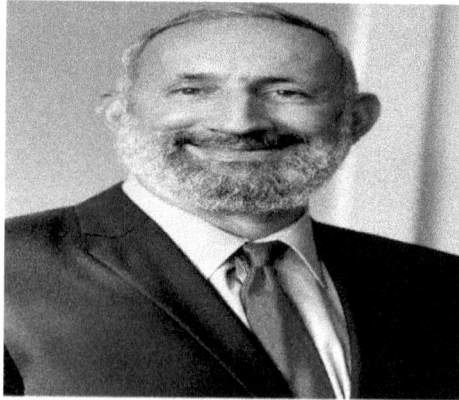

Brian D. Lerner is an Immigration Lawyer and runs a National Immigration Law Firm for nearly 30 years. He is an attorney who is a certified specialist that might help in Immigration & Nationality Law as issued by the California State Bar, Board of Legal Specialization. Attorney Lerner is an expert in Immigration Law, Removal and Deportation, Citizenship, Waiver and Appeals.

He has been a licensed attorney since 1992 and started the Law Offices of Brian D. Lerner, APC. The immigration practice consists of Immigration and Nationality Law, and everything involved with and regarding immigration which includes citizenship, investment visas, family and employment visas, removal and deportation hearings, appeals, waivers, adjustment, consulate processing and all types of immigration and citizenship matters.

He has represented clients from all over the U.S. and in many countries around the world. One side of his practice is dedicated to keeping people in the U.S. and fighting for their immigration rights, while another side is to get people back who have been deported and removed from the U.S.

Also, there is the affirmative part of Immigration Law which Brian Lerner has helped numerous people come into the U.S. on business visa, investment visas, student visas, fiancee and marriage visas, religious visas and many more. Attorney Lerner has helped immigrants who are victims of crime and domestic violence or ones that are married to abusers.

In other words, Attorney Lerner has a firm that helps people all over the U.S. He has dedicated significant time to preparing numerous petitions and applications for you to get at a fraction of the price of hiring an attorney. He says it is the next best thing to a real attorney because they are real petitions prepared by an expert.